The To Sound

Publication of this book was supported by a grant from
The Greenwall Fund of The Academy of American Poets.

The To Sound

Eric Baus

to Deb,

you're never left behind!

Love, Eric

Verse Press • Amherst, MA

Published by Verse Press
www.versepress.org

Library of Congress Cataloging-in-Publication Data

Baus, Eric.
  The to sound : poems / Eric Baus.-- 1st ed.
     p. cm.
  ISBN 0-9723487-4-3 (alk. paper)
  I. Title.
  PS3602.A97T6 2003
  811'.6--dc21

                                        2003012682

The To Sound is the winner of the 2002 Verse Prize, selected by Forrest Gander.

Designed and composed by J. Johnson
Text set in Garamond. Display set in Trade Gothic Bold Condensed No. 20.
Cover art: *Swan Greed: for Raymond Roussel* by Elizabeth Zechel. Courtesy of the artist.

9 8 7 6 5 4 3 2 1

First Edition

for George Kalamaras

Acknowledgments

Thanks to the editors of the following magazines for publishing pieces of this work: *Baffling Combustions, Can We Have Our Ball Back, Castagraf, Colorado Review, Combo, Comet, Cul-de-qui* (U.K.), *Facture, First Intensity, Hambone, Key Satch(el), Phoebe, Quarter After Eight, 3rd Bed, Third Coast, Untitled: A Magazine of Prose Poetry, Verse,* and *Vert.* Portions were published as the chapbooks *the space between magnets* (Diaeresis Press) and *a swarm in the aperture* (Margin to Margin). An epistolary collaboration with George Kalamaras prompted several of the poems in *your recently collected saliva.* Thanks to my friends, family, and teachers for their generosity and support.

Contents

the space between magnets

THE SISTERS OF THE BROKEN CANDLE

covered every window in the house with x-rays of my bandaged eye.

"working backwards from the sky" says she follows every fissure until it's time for the stitches to come out. When something falls you should pick it up.

"spilled sand and lamplight" has been my sister for a while now.

They say we are slivered glass. Fluttered numbers and milk. Flickers sutured in skin.

They tried to convince me that half the word filament is night. Every rattled out lightbulb means a brother's pillow is burning.

We all watch the clock. Eyes running out of aluminum.

They wanted me to hold the bird calmly

until its wings atrophied, until my hands filled with moot feathers. I remember something flapping. I forgot where I buried the bones.

Dear Birds, There is no natural light in here.

Your hungers are folded in half. My kitchen is full of kale smoke and cinders. Take whatever you find. When you said there would be stars I couldn't hear the s. I apologize for using my museum voice. I'm sorry for all the photographs I took. All of your gambling debts are forgiven.

Dearest Sister, I wanted to hear about your travels.

Call it "medicine for a scorched turbine," a little phosphorus sprinkled in my morning cereal. I've decided to make peace with the pigeons. Thank you for the gracious gift of magnets, my blood is pumping much slower, although I burned my tongue on the aspirin-coated toast you sent. Did you send the aspirin-coated toast? Was that aspirin mixed in with the ashes?

I was thinking *birds with extremely long necks*

and my sister sees   *I was using words I didn't know*   she nods and we know
    a voice   my mouth uses rain to say   the body is a sequence

    that counts
    as it moves   the body is a museum
           where we apologize   for our voices

        birds with inky wings
        flapping above the fire

    my sister was thinking
    a dim constellation   *my body is rain*
                     wired together

she nods once because   a sequential feeling is what counts
we are half-sisters twice   birds with extremely long necks

    using our indoor voice   using words we can't see

I apologize for my voice turning to dust

   what I'm saying is   *a dim asterisk in my lips*
   born from the weather

     of a blistered   tongue
      thought   torn   in the shape of birds

my sister opens her eyes to say
something is always burning

she thinks   *the sun dims*
when anything falls   and I see

every rattled out lightbulb means   *my sister's pillow is smoke*
shadow of cranes

half the word filament is night

Dear Birds, Nothing works the same way twice.

If I say *my eyes are quotation marks pulled across the sky,* I mean the way a beaten wing is parallel to treading water. I'm sorry for transcribing the incendiary tenor you never wanted read into your movements. I've exposed all my film. This morning I found bits of your letters in the newspaper, clustered around the four-color pictures. It was funny how you made magenta bleed from the image of the eclipse. To prove a point I circled all the letters in CASSIOPEIA in the metro section. I'm tired of breathing through my sleeve in a rented room.

DEAREST SISTER, IF IT'S A MATTER OF LEARNING HOW TO TIE THE RIGHT KNOT

or always building in a slip big enough for only your own index, why is there so much orphaned thread on my body, so much faux lunar dust still left on my fingers? If you are going to tell me it's a matter of breathing from the diaphragm and counting to four, you'll have to forgive my absence of perfectly phrased clippings to back you up. It's the third of February and I'm already into my paperback voice. Nothing works.

my sister was thinking   *I was a scatter of birds*
    placing flames   next to each other

      if she said   the tongue   is a furnace
my mouth was burning   splinters

      so to speak   a surface
    shaping names   using my physical voice

if I said   my fingers are ellipses,
    a fluorescence, fissures

she was looking for some handwriting
    to pull across her lips

      I was working in the soundbox
working in the pipes   under my breath

if I said my hands are   blistered filters
    pulled across   my eyes

I was using the gape   seeing the word sun
in my sister's mouth

Dear Birds, I'm running out of numbers.

Whenever I look at the clock it's always turning 1:23 or 5:55. My mouth is always a three or a one. Everything I see wants to be shaped like your wings when you said *I last saw her out in the rain.* She said she got lost for several pages, thinking glass was the x for my outstretched arms. Incidentally, she was unimpressed by the house of cards you constructed out of litmus paper. We are all so far from home. I remember the way she'd hold a parasol against the sun, watching carp lunge onto rocks, like being able to walk made us the solution for water. I don't know how many times I've called a stranger sister.

DEAREST SISTER, THANKS FOR LEAVING ME SPACE TO SIGN MY FULL NAME IN YOUR ABSENCE.

I looked so hard I thought my neck was permanently stretched, that all the children on my block would always have elongated glances. I sent you postcards from every skylit exit. Did you get the one when I thought the word sun in my mouth could keep us both warm? We both know glare is not enough border: bending light is a form of precision. I've got my "dealing from the bottom of the deck" goggles on. Today I drew chalk outlines around my eyes. I can treat all this traffic like a single evening voice.

WHILE THE SOMNAMBULIST EXPLAINS THE PROPER WAY TO CARVE THE EYES FROM A PIGEON,

I ask in my indoor voice what it means to extract your own teeth during sleep.

He thinks about the three minutes he stopped breathing in saltwater. Closing his lids at fish. Wondering why his shirt felt like skin.

I try to explain why gravity always wins. How lightning is rhetorical. The way "weight takes over a wing" comes to my lips when I pass a downed powerline.

He speaks softly with empty sleeves. Says a bird losing altitude is a new kind of rain. Roughly equivalent to the fluid in my ears.

Dear Birds, You can say I contact whoever is in the memorized room,

"the shade my mouth bent open" or "handfuls of sugar untouched in an abdomen." I was fully articulated when you said *this voice is changing, find me a new skin* like my index was sound, like my blankest card said "surface worker." I was solving for your absence, a shift in the tinted angles sounding out your edges. The translations you left on my doorstep were clear, but the passage you call "self-portrait with wounded docent" is a little oblique. I'm afraid you'll have to build another machine to explain yourself.

Dearest Sister, If all stars are syllogisms,

tell me what to say before I know what I've seen. You say we hum
to make our names translucent, to keep the constellations moving.
Call me "a bell to warn the birds" when a drift of one eye means
enough letters for flight. In the landscape of your predicates I'm
CASSIOPEIA, hair made of glass, and a burning wing. I don't need
to dot a line through my lips to know where you've gone. If typing
is talking with a single sound, I can always tell when you're thinking
of the sun.

Wondering why her shoes felt like skin

she asked what animal left lines under her eyes.

We matched wingprints to moths burned in gaslight.

Chalked it up to the dangers of oxygen. Hydrogen to Helium.
What the sun does.

We watched the scar on the palm of her left hand. The way
bleeding thumbs breed during sleep.

Our compass couldn't detect the moment a blister bloomed. Our
abacus long since retired to the house of wooden fingers.

I slept in her arms for a week.

Whispered *ashes of shoulder* to the bottoms of her heels. Embers
lighting through her throat.

Dear Birds, I was walking under the radar when I heard your older voice

using the electrical storm to say *deliver us from one who evicts.* You asked how much more you could hear if I didn't know your language. I was crossed out in the digits, sufficiently in love with my own cochlea to leave it to archeology. I'm sorry for your dizziness, I know you meant the lightning rhetorically, how everything insists on falling. I was watching where it charges, the sky a skipped frame in my peripheral. The way I asked you to say what you saw made me blind for half the morning. You are roughly equivalent to my lips turning red, talking to the walls with a headful of soot.

Dearest Sister, Sugar is suffering somewhere in water.

When I'm talking to myself in the rain I'm speaking to your frequency. Today your voice was on the radio saying *Wolfgang Amadeus Mozart died of rheumatic fever* like it was the last digit of Pi. What do you want me to do with that? I'm thinking through a skin of wet cloth. I'm an exponent of everything you've ever said. I can feel your wavelengths growing in every bite of apple, every damp step of ash.

she lies   skylit   under bones   branches
splinted limbs   a splintered fluorescence   in an ash of breath

you've been my sister   a prism
  for a while now   spilled sand   and lamplight
     in the bends of my back

she says

her light enters   asks *where it goes*
through an abdomen   *when it falls*

the space between jaws

       says
       take my throat out
       while you're at it

or *panes of stained glass*

in a burnt husk
     of breath   *take*
       my fish
       my foot
she was   a winter's worth of hum in   *my ghost*
     birdbones
   born

a lungful of cinders
     in a house between atmospheres

       don't even go back
       for your pillow

Dear Birds, I'm straining through your lenses,

a string of your voicebox in everything I sift. When you said *breathe me another grasp of ash, crush me for my blueprints* I slipped out of the crescendo, a MARCO POLO asleep in your sonar. I was using my magnifying voice, wondering why my sieve calls your silhouette a frame, if I was moth enough to hear through your capitalized wings. When you said your densest glass was melting, I could see the place between matrix and maxillary in your brightest mouth, I could feel my pupils shrinking.

Dearest Sister, What is the difference between "an instrument of revision"

and "laughing in the water lungs" if I say *I'm talking to the back of my throat?* I mean the way you keep my head still to see whatever is nearest. When you erased all the letters in scaffolding and blew away the chalkdust, I was unable to explain "twenty stethoscopes and closing," as if wind were a form of eating. You say *something is always burning,* but where is my genus, my species of kindling?

THE HOUSE OF SLEEPING CHILDREN

twisted in bed eating starfruit some small boy dropped from the sky said he invented helixes nightly the house of sleeping children thinned by the sun close your eyes said the international sign for helixes nightly said hum the house of sleeping children kept track of themselves spiral staircases spoke of the body said hum star-faced helixes nightly the house of sleeping children evening crawling back from the tonsils fall forward star-faced dropped from the sky the house of sleeping children helixes nightly

Dear Birds, There is still some weather here,

a splinter of your alphabet in everything I read. This morning you said *when weight takes over a wing two brushfires are canceled.* That's what I mean when I'm talking in circles. Your vibrations are exceptional, the half-glints and cellophane, but I can't be your magic eight ball today. My wisdom teeth are gone, bronzed and dropped down the sink. I'm hiding from the sky, my own brand of photosynthephobia. You saw through my darkroom voice the way circular breathing makes flight possible. You said you can see anything through my swollen eye.

Dearest Sister, Let's not pretend there are no bad questions.

Just because you're halfway through the night doesn't mean the world has to split down the center. When you showed me how to hold an umbrella upside down, gathering light, there wasn't time to draw a new map, to talk me through another set of teeth. We've covered this ground before, the place between opacity and oracle in my library mouth. If I'm playing to the angles of an empty house, give me some feedback from your fleshed out shadows.

If a Sleeper Moves into Her Own Snow

she lifts a burning word and "lightning escapes." She says her matches in different boxes of the sternum. Hers is not always a stopping silhouette, every singe in the quiet sliding off.

She says she likes to take the little words out. She would say "down in clock" to count a flutter of fingers. To name an ache in her covers she would say "cellophane," and she would know cold and crystal.

If a sleeper moves into her own snow she moves from a blinking place, the border between prism and mirror in the corner of her eyes. She moves through sheeted lid, through the unfurled squint of night. If a sleeper says the chest is a place just to step from, all the little words tilde in her lashes.

She asked herself after her birds stilled, after her air emptied of useful plumage. She asked after herself, even in the corner of her eyes, she asked after all her little words. She asked if a sleeper has to say anything to her own snow.

The chest is a place, she says, to count the little words out. A blinking place to name, and a mirror. She says her matches with a covered cold and crystal. She is always the flicker in a stilled silhouette.

She moves and "lightning escapes" to say anything blinking, to count all the cellophane in her words. She would not always be sheeted a sleeper, she would say a box to step from after her birds unfurled.

DEAR BIRDS, THE RAIN WAS ON TIME.

I couldn't exhale long enough to explain my delays, to spell out why I'd been watching the clock, waiting for both arms to align. I couldn't tell you in the smoky corner how the angle of my knife to your empty glasses was like holding dowsing rods over my head. I'm lost in my own percentages, looking to slake a thirst in the gradations of your hunger.

Dearest Sister, I'm sorry I used the wrong words to call you,

I thought anything with one syllable would speak to your shadow. I don't need to trace your outline in my fogged up windows to watch water break in the bodies around me. When you said you were tired of living like a silhouette I could feel every naked bulb burning in the house. I could taste the mercury frozen in all my fillings.

WHEN THE SOMNAMBULIST WENT BACK TO SLEEP

he did so with an incomplete knowledge of the incendiary
vocabulary of snails.

He asked to be called "peristalsis." I said "phosphorus."

With the gift of slowness came other offerings. Seeds burning in a
belly. Handfuls of sugar untouched in an abdomen.

He showed me how to extract heat from electrical outlets. I spent
the extra money on sunglasses.

His was not a stillness. He subscribed to the motion picture theory
of stasis. Each word a frozen flame.

I could stay up for days enumerating the movements in his eyelids.

The pain in my sheets won't go away.

I am caught in him like a moment of sodium.

your recently collected saliva

SORRY FOR MY ABSENCE OF LINES, MY BREATH HAS
TIGHTENED OVER TWO HOURS BECOMING HELICAL
ENOUGH TO INFEST THE EXACT SCENT OF YOUR SPINE.

I am curious about your veiled inclusion, or spurious lack thereof, of iodine in the forms you filled out. Yes, the salt you sent in your recently collected saliva includes this "necessary nutrient" but the extraction process is as long as the morning is phosphor. Was this unsifted sodium sent as an oblique reference to unindexed history, an aside describing passive resistance to the blood always pooling in the sea's sink? Are you saying the gesture in a harvest of ash can be applied to the fall of colloidal grains? Have you drawn a circle in the sand with an x?

I am writing to you from the most public library in the world.

Your papers have fully arrived.

The critique of geometry is endless.

I am metric to your wounds.

Earlier, when I quoted my regional correspondent calling sunshine "a syntactically inferior form of transportation," I was referring to the way your light splits my tongue in four directions, delaying the, causing an a in my of. Yes, you can say I "use whatever is in the memorized room," but I can't help feeling we're trading our primary feathers for illustrations of a paperback island.

It is official. I have been your sister since January 15th, 1995.

The pulp in your podium has fully arrived the remains in of.

THE WORD MOON GOT TETANUS.

No one noticed until starcharts were found covered in oxidized blood. Improperly folded. Constellations scattered in the sky. We had no idea an eclipse was the event we'd been circled together to discuss. Something was burning. Something was always burning. We couldn't see. Staring through the holes in our hands with the holes in our eyes. Someone objected to our use of the word moon. They said it stood for nothing. We clasped hands: "You are right. The word moon said empty the etymology of bodies." Alone with the night sky. Cinematographers framed fingers around stars.

Someone poked straws in contact lenses to shrink the swelling. I knew better staring through the small ends of funnels. I met the mapmaker halfway from the observatory. A handful of burning starchart sifting through her arms: "The problem is not gravity lack of light or the red shifting clouds that roll over our heads." She asked the difference between growing a beard and not shaving. I chose the latter and grass grew around my ankles. We spoke like matches in mirrors. Everything bounced back twice as bright and upside down.

The line between astronomy and cutting the grass grew thicker every time we tried to remove it. The word moon stood in someone. Held us inverted by our ankles from a canopy of trees to see how the moon looked through the optic nerve. The optic nerves were offended by this gesture. Showed cowboy films from the fifties. Several members of the party were injured by arrows. They showed a documentary on the voyages of Columbus. Several members of the party got scurvy. The freelance mapmaker worked for days. Named new cities after bones. Crowds of pointed fingers turned to dust. For miles around teeth dropped to the ground. Maps blankened. The word moon burned holes in our eyes.

I AM BUILDING A BODY OUT OF PAPER, SPLAY, AND
SPLICE.

You write *I am the one after zero* to displace my scattered breath,
to shake off every landscape, but what does it mean to correspond
through glass, to continue a critique of accumulated angles?

Rendering clutter, you say our dialogue is "buzzed with the" or "a
twin of approximate glint," but I'm concerned about curl, the arc of
letters in elongate and distend. Undertone or puncture.

Your letters turn to means in the thinking dust.

Remember in the house between cinder and flare, where your worn
parchment was a split open rain, the straightest cut of stars, my
tongue wrapped in sparks? You could say I bend the law of threes to
cross-section that count.

You could shape my mouth to believe in the body, descent, and
sugar, but why replace my tongue with test flint, why cast an
understudy to pronounce our gravel stone?

ARCHITECTURE BASED ON THE STRUCTURE OF THE SMALL INTESTINE WAS INDEED A BAD IDEA.

Someone interrupted from the back of the cathedral. Asked the mapmaker why he took great pains in erasing all the letters in pomegranate. Why he blew on the chalkboard gently, as if his wind were a form of eating.

The cartographer's stomach rumbled. He was not really a cartographer. He only wanted a world without flying ants. A world entirely of insects unwinged. Apteroids. Birds having the wings elementary. A place where turkeys chew bone under the silt of rivers. Although the air smoked a hug or handshake still seemed appropriate. The failed interlocutor was characteristically silent. The failed translator was unable or unwilling or unable to explain. No one argued aloud. Every time the mapmaker spoke the index fingerprint of his left hand grew a little dimmer. The fault lines were all framed. Filled in with soot. The curve of the mapmaker's calf looked like the coastline of California.

All the fresh fruit had rotted. The convenience store clerk walked out of the cathedral. Tired and impatient and angry that his sink dripped all night. Everyone coughed at the same time. The six rows of sleeping children piled up behind the organ.

Young intellectuals in black robes distributed pamphlets. Questioned the ethics of cartography. A mathematician went mad. Screamed at the dentist sitting next to him about the importance of filling in every crack. The cartographer tried to convince everyone that someday the basement would be finished. Two plain-clothed physicians made everyone line up for x-rays before they could leave. Waved compasses over every child's chest.

THERE APPEARS TO BE DIAGNOSTIC FRICTION IN YOUR AMBLYOPIA, YOUR PATCHED OFF FLIGHT.

The corrected version begins: *if a seed powders to husk in the bowel of* . . . not *the x-rays came back blank, the coral hull is groaning* . . .

Follow the pointer with all your moths closed.

Crack this grounded star like so: *as a symbol of my capitalized wing* [better one?] *as a dented speech of teeth* [better two?]

Your vowels have been spreading since I notarized the "ancient am" under your arm, and your tilted diction suggests a torch of arid bladder syndrome. The crunching in of hosts.

Jean-Michel Basquiat's "Anybody Speaking Words" (1982, acrylic and oil paintstick on canvas, 96 by 61.5 inches) is perhaps the best glottal stop for your repealed gloss, your nitrogen highness. As I'm sure this piece clearly demonstrates, the centrifugal swerve in your third opera is almost entirely crossed, an impossibly intoned operation.

I assuage you, this aphasia will swoon.

the accomplished alchemist becomes blue scales on the belly of a sturgeon trapped in the waves of the Mediterranean Sea. Becomes aluminum under the gold plating of two spoons crossed in the open casket of a quail's egg. Becomes the sweetness of milk dissolved in an injured physician's cup of coffee.

She hides in the long wet hairs of his black handlebar mustache. Escapes into the air when he coughs a cough of black smoke into the air. Flushed like a goose stumbled into flight. Flecked with buckshot.

He is clenched for revenge after lifetimes of stifled rage. He is in hate with the parentheses around his left fist. He is a sporting man, with a belly full of scrambled eggs and breath as thick as butter, night, blood.

Of course she runs into the streets where the black stones are passing out. Of course she finds a blind corner, pauses to think of x-ray machines and calculators that conspire against her in laboratories before bringing a plumed bottle of water up to the hole in her chest.

She can feel the row of fluorescent lights in her spine. She can feel a handful of sugar suffering in water.

The physician is twenty stethoscopes away and closing with two rusty spoons nearly crossed into an x.

Suddenly her water becomes unfair. Breaks simply in the bodies around him. Suddenly becomes unfair. Leaves a pile of rotten caviar. A shoeful of sucrose. A single peacock feather riddled with lice. A fisherman swoons poisoned by tainted poultry. The physician draws an x in the rubble with a knuckle from his right hand. Fishes for a ghost until dawn. But the alchemist is accomplished. Her grains scattered by his heavy breath.

Twenty blocks away a little girl throws a firecracker at the feet of a little boy. Gold sparks burning the short blond hairs of his legs.

Thanks for grasping the pigeons I sutured to your lining.

I was trying to pronounce our science quieter than skin. To be awash in surface. The stretching out of chords.

I am worried about your embedded bout of disavowal. The submerged magenta hidden under your blue. The arteries of am or spilled tongue of a.

Everything I say is part sound rain. Half flayed iris. A flutter or umbra in the house of wound beginning.

The contractions accrue.

Do I really need to talk myself transparent? Can you still see my fingers through your cellophane dome, your most lucent ceiling? Hinging each clear to glass, you are twice my projected image. A singular moth emitting in factions.

You say we are extracted from the underscore, partially sounded grain. To express our collapsed service. To represent a divided hive. You say the chest is a place just to step from, but I have found a crushed the in my lungs. A cyst in the flight of my buried in.

Become a pinhole, you called, turning to sparrows, but my detritus had already changed to dirt, all my alembics slowly went box. I am filtered from your chimera. A tincture in the progress of your aviary voice. Trying to pollinate a stop and its edges.

the thing I do is speaking

I CAN'T PICTURE MYSELF,

but I know my name. It is simpler than the accomplished place I am outside. Please, anything except my tin, the tiny cup. You are not my mouth but it sounds like you, the illustrations I picture. I know how to read signs. I have flames. Do not touch the bees. Dissolved in the dome, the lost signals form. I think, I remember, and I am still. The vapors remain themselves.

AT FIRST I WAS QUIET,

keeping track of myself. You said you consider yourself bees, tin bees, and bees. I watched the ground weigh itself, lured to the ground. I don't want to say anything about us, what we are made of, or the tin cup the teller's mouth ruined. When I can't think of another, I use the word signal. You would sound so good beside my name. It is pictorial. From the painting. I can't place you. How do you know my work? You can touch anything except for me. Come outside, please. You have strayed in my mouth for so long.

Between your sounds,

I am not quiet. Remember the place that I am. I was named. I have form. I want to watch the work as it speaks, but I can only hear my own signal. You were lured to the bees. I use the word picture to think of something else. Please, remain yourself. I think I and picture you. Touch. Read. Remember, you illustrated me. Lost signal. I never knew how to ground. You stray in the reeds. I think I am here to see something else.

At first you were miniature,

floating outside. Now it sounds like I can touch the ground. The sun has been practicing those tiny flames all night. You approach yourself, dissolving. I say I am simpler than my form sounds in your mouth. You are not not quiet. You accomplish yourself silently. I watch my tin, the tiny flames. You launching into you. When you are in my place, I hear myself outside. The gasses go by but I am grounded.

The last time you assembled,

you said I was pictorial. You are not pictorial and I am like sod for
a miniature of flames. Touch the dome, it is not still, the sun gasses
go by outside. Please repair my mouth, I need it to work. I am so
sorry I ruined your bees, I was lost in the signal. I don't remember
anything except the tin cup sounds like you. I never knew how to
whistle. Between your dissolve and my frame, a paper buries itself.
How did you fit inside those tiny illustrations? I am afraid I can't
read. Come closer, I have been tuning all night. I can tell you were
moving behind my ear.

a swarm in the aperture

THE SISTERS OF THE GATHERED FILAMENTS

tuned in another phase of static. "three parts spine" called me
placeholder.

"begging bowl of ash" took me for a burned atlas. Interference.
Said *star this ground for cracking.*

"dye breaks the surface" opened like a sieve sentence. Fell to
nearest water swept. Froze my dearest splash and voltage.

They say the diameter of a sibling's finger is the thickest shard of
glass. The compass rose a sleeve of scales.

We are leavened in atmosphere. Figures for a darkroom voice.
Bodies sketched in silt.

Dear Birds, I'm broken to my circuits,

a shatter of your syntax in everything I split. This morning I woke
up in your prism voice saying *bind me to your pages, keep the blinds
closed.* When you said my orbit in the current tongue was done, I
was frozen in the clutter, a camera failing to close both eyes. You say
your wings will reproduce well, but why are there so many cracks in
my monocle, so much secondhand ink still left on my instruments?
If we are lost to the same circumference, siblings of stranded glass,
why can't I diagram the phrasing of your limbs?

DEAREST SISTER, MY MOST BURIED WIRES TELL ME
WE ARE THINKING OF THE SAME FISH.

Talking to ourselves in tandem. The scab on your left hand a polar
star, an opening in rock, and a splash of weight. Tonight I found
a torn photo of your palms on my thinnest sounding board, my
cellophane scroll. As you etched "the statue takes a skin" in my
greenest screen, I crossed myself after every negation saying *build me
out of fallen leaves, barter me for driftwood.* When you scattered iron
filings on the lines in my cheeks, I could feel the exact temperature
in the house of bundled fibers, I could hear your oldest rain hitting
the ground.

She said I was tired of living like a sieve in a house between atmospheres,

talking out the texture of her mouth in an unfiltered room. *Call me the rule of broken threes, a swarm in the aperture, a split in the even listening.*

She rubbed handfuls of charcoal through my hollowed out cheeks.

I found so much smolder in the same number of steps, so much undeclared tinder in the slits of her teeth.

She said *if hunger was just one word, whatever comes next is a bridge.* When she blew out all the fallen candles, I felt to see if the door was warm.

What I'm asking for is a fish border, a fence equal to her scattered breath.

Dear Birds, Thanks for the construction paper crown,

you know how much a consensus means to me. When you closed your eyes the radio said *the spine is a spool of filaments.* I'm the docent of everything you've ever sewn. If it's a matter of squinting at a fettered sun, I'm spilled through your number lines, wondering why my tongue is so shadow, why hand is snow in my spelling voice. Say what you want about my moving parts, I'm not going to throw sticks in your shade.

Dearest Sister, Your voice is volume times ash.

When I heard you got your vitamins through half-drawn curtains,
I could feel your deepest crescent turning, I could trace your
trajectory to a split open listening, the straightest cut of parchment.
It took me all night to decode the pile of flint you put under my
pillow. What do you mean *keep me with my splinted s, render me into
your hand?* I'm sorry I didn't splice your flames, I was blinded in the
projection booth.

THE SLEEPER'S BREATH BECOMES HELICAL ENOUGH TO INFEST THE EXACT SCENT OF SHROUD.

Becomes the frequency for *window pulled inward, thrust of arms glancing*. Becomes an aching ring virulent with pitch, scalded solid as nest cloth lodged in the chimney of the house of failing tendons. Strings a note flatter than three birds trapped in a twist of soot blackened hair. Talks back behind her throat, scraping seeds through her bowels at the thought of sewing stones. Divides in the utterance of crushed chalk, spilled in her sinuses as the steepest vertigo ever spelled.

Dear Birds, "a lisp in the surface" is the quietest sister.

Tell me house of splintered voice. Align to her gloss: *if the bluest see through kindling, if a cinder finds its way.* Call isotope alarm, the antidote for oxygen. Wake me to her longitude, a safer razor than speech. Now I'm frozen jawbone, talking picture theory, seeing the sediment in a sudden drop of sternum.

Dearest Sister, When I told the radio I was sorry

I was using my dowsing voice to sound your broken water. A paper crown tracing your nods to thinking dust, the smallest feather tools. The serum you smeared on my antennae was enough to triangulate, to find your faintest mercator, but I can't see a difference between the shore, spilled iodine, and fissures in a sinking craft. I'm marking every corollary, blowing on the husk of a burned out circuit.

THE SLEEPER DEVELOPS IN THE CHORDS OF MY THROAT.

To collapse our necks with glass. To pronounce the latent hive in her chest.

Look we are a loom and a fissure straying.

The voice you hear means blind or ghost. Threads.

If I tunnel or extract to pronounce our blanks.

Your medicine is a negative mouth. A still between frames. Skipping.

She uses her radio voice to assess the tension in a phonograph.

To collapse her frames with utterance. To assess the embedded throat.

I am a chord and husk of that gloss.

She develops straying retina and all her tones stammer.

We are threaded in thirds. Film slivers. Transistor medicine.

I am the retina and throat of that ghost. Recorded in her blanks.

She enters through the fissures. The vagrant space between our eyes.

To pronounce the blank in her mouth.

We develop in the space between revolving and breath.

Gloss in the chords. Detached.

I am a hive and shard of that voice.

If she speaks slowly to collapse her veins with smoke.

I see nothing but shimmers. A negative mouth. Skipping frames.

Between a tunnel of blank and running. She extracts my projector voice.

To say that ghost stammers. That gloss stings. Transistor.

Dear Birds, Your worn parchment was just one word.

Thread from the docent of precious gifts, sewing skins wrapped in string or a flock in the chimney. I hear the place between algorithm and aperture is the most curved cup of sand, but why is my hourglass so full of water, why are your residues always clear? If all the openings in the building know the exact temperature of my tongue am I stenciling holes on a sleeping stenographer? If I blink my adopted eye while you fall to the ground my sister can see the seams on your wings.

Dearest Sister, You say slip and score is a way of closing broken

or gather debris as the rendering appendage asks what a foot of splintered wood means. I saw *the throat is a fuselage* in a twist of blind fibers, then your letter was stamped on my spine. While you assembled the reflection of my bending elbow from cracked glass I couldn't tell whether soma meant body or sleep, if your language could hold two words for converge. I am scattered in your pages, a handful of litmus in the space between wires.

TO COLLIDE A BODY UNUSED TO DROPPING

she writes me as "the breathing machine sketch" or "carves of my wooden."

She says *in the museum of articulation, sister minus sister equals brother* and I see her thinking mouth is a way of being modular.

If multiples mean a shrunken form of seeing. If three begets a second kind of speech.

She moves another mirror to track the closer phosphors: *that's not the only facing way, turned out eye.* Every letter standing in a slit open rain.

She thinks "paraphrase the medicine" is an instrument of remission. Talking to a half-heard sibling in the skipped frames.

DEAR BIRDS, WHEN YOU SAW ETYMOLOGY AS A SWELLING EPICENTER,

I wondered how your letters would sound if I spelled your flares locus or kept the points plotted on crumpled paper. If half the word floater is ghost cursive, a way of asking for three more minutes of filament in the last watt of a lightbulb, where is the gradient in my pinhole glasses, my mouth cloaked in mumbling? You said hearing me talk was loaning flour to sugar. I'm all out of order, looking through the blanks where your eyes used to be.

Dearest Sister, I can feel your digits in the stoppings of my watch,

a cast of your shadow in everything I count. You write me as "asterisks sparring over unclaimed zero" but why is your appendix so full of holes, why am I frozen whenever you speak? When you used your lightest graphite to tell me *parlance is leaky, grieving rock,* a thin line was drawn across all my divisors. When you asked me to watch the loa and lobe in your cargo ear, you sounded like knuckle was tonsil, as if finger meant fissure.

THE SOMNAMBULIST SAYS THE OLDEST SWALLOW IN HIS THROAT HAS FINALLY GONE AQUA,

and I hear *he is stretched over the injured skin of lost and familiar waters.* A radio for sounding the most brittle blue.

I was wounded in the particulate. Closed like any other cloud to broken ground.

He says we are cleft in a house of removing signals. Folding rafters in the permafrost.

I bring up the fluid in a bird to call his surface plastic. To say the quietest gesture is falling from a mouth.

Wings bundled or glass

Though we build a smaller breach in clinging.

How circuitous attacks. A reverb strung through doubled arms, talking down a wall of stunted endings.

How literally to be in that strand or thinking voice, a tangle gone reverse.

As stumbled loops alleviate. As paraffin or clone.

Who wrought these frayed flight lines. A bubble steep from speaking its parabola.

If parallel suggests a hidden vein. If heat attracts a single word for sunshine.

Tell me, bird loops, suggest a lens or hide a clenched word for sender, how sun finds the most circuitous quail.

Siblings bleached in a single cell. The redundant wings we assemble.

the to sound

The to sound

To look out a window is to want to be on the side of the birds.

You arrange your arms so the distance is clear.

If the entire was wound. Breathed glass. A tooth embedded so far it burst.

A cut of your cloth to negate every saw.

You are the one after zero. The sister of a. Bird tuned to ash.

To pronounce your medicine in my mouth.

I know I can never understand the. Even if the was powder on my lips.

Unacknowledged and disguised as *O Zero, et tu?*

If my eye could stay glass. Breathe. And stem.

Can a wound enter the was? Can one entire turn?

Stay. I know the tired sound.

To look out a window is to be embedded inside birds.

If I could amplify your glass. Atone for the sound of my incessant lips.

You are a. Too. Tuned to has. Ash.

You are the you and. The to sound. The utter the.

If I have to spit out all my teeth to stay in the.

The. Is it all to say the weight of the?

If I could stay lost to sound. If a single eye could say two.

To breathe glass. To unwind a wing.

To say the entire wound as window. Stone turned to sound.

If the sting unwound itself as sleet. As rain in the cut stem.

If the window to pronounce magnifies.

You are the one after end. The burned bird I woke up in.